Exploring Space

Journey through the solar system and beyond

ENCYCLOPÆDIA

CHICAGO   LONDON   NEW DELHI   PARIS   SEOUL   SYDNEY   TAIPEI   TOKYO

Exploring Space

INTRODUCTION

What do stars really look like?

Could you live on Venus? Are aliens waiting for us in outer space?

What did astronomers study hundreds of years ago?

In *Exploring Space,* you'll discover answers to these questions and many more. Through pictures, articles, and fun facts, you'll travel across time, visit outer space, meet fascinating people, and investigate strange and wonderful things.

To help you on your journey, we've provided the following guideposts in *Exploring Space*:

■ **Subject Tabs**—The colored box in the upper corner of each right-hand page will quickly tell you the article subject.

■ **Search Lights**—Try these mini-quizzes before and after you read the article and see how much—*and how quickly*—you can learn. You can even make this a game with a reading partner. (Answers are upside down at the bottom of one of the pages.)

■ **Did You Know?**—Check out these fun facts about the article subject. With these surprising "factoids," you can entertain your friends, impress your teachers, and amaze your parents.

■ **Picture Captions**—Read the captions that go with the photos. They provide useful information about the article subject.

■ **Vocabulary**—New or difficult words are in **bold type**. You'll find them explained in the Glossary at the end of the book.

■ **Learn More!**—Follow these pointers to related articles in the book. These articles are listed in the Table of Contents and appear on the Subject Tabs.

Britannica®
LEARNING LIBRARY

Have a great trip!

Exploring Space
TABLE OF CONTENTS

SEARCH LIGHT

Which of these things do astronomers study?
- stars
- planets
- moons
- astronauts
- comets

Studying the Stars

Look at the sky. What do you see?

If it's day you'll see the Sun. If it's night you'll see the Moon. And if the sky is clear you'll see stars. In big cities you may see only a few hundred stars. But out in the country or on the ocean you'll see many thousands. You may even see planets and, if you're lucky, a **comet**.

There are people who look at the sky for hours and hours, night after night. They study the stars, the planets, and other objects in the sky. These people are called "astronomers." The word "astronomy" comes from the Greek for "star" and "arrangement."

Astronomers study the universe in many different ways. Some watch faraway objects. Others work in **laboratories**, where they look at samples of **meteorites**, rocks from the Moon, and space **debris** from other planets. Some try to make models of different objects people have studied.

Not all astronomers get paid for the work they do. Some do it for a hobby. Such people are called "amateur astronomers."

How do astronomers study objects that are millions, even billions, of miles away? They use powerful telescopes that make things look large enough to be seen in detail. Some telescopes are small enough to be held in the hand. Others are as big as a school bus!

LEARN MORE! READ THESE ARTICLES...
COPERNICUS • SOLAR SYSTEM • UNIVERSE

Answer: They study all of these except for astronauts.

Infinite Space

The universe is a vast **expanse** of space that contains all matter and energy, from the smallest particle to the biggest galaxy. It contains all the planets, the Sun, stars, asteroids, our Milky Way galaxy, and all the other galaxies too.

No one knows how big the universe is. Astronomers believe that it is still growing outward in every direction.

How did it all begin? No one knows that for sure either.

Most scientists believe that at first everything was one incredibly solid, heavy ball of matter. This ball exploded billions of years ago—and the universe was born. The moment of this explosion is called the "big bang." It is from this moment that time began.

After the explosion the early universe was small and extremely hot. As it cooled, it expanded and pieces spread out. Small pieces formed the basic

SEARCH LIGHT

If the universe is still growing, is it moving toward or away from the Earth?

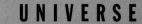

elements hydrogen and helium. Other pieces began to join together, and objects began to form. Over billions of years the objects became galaxies, stars, and planets.

This is still only a theory, an idea. But different parts of it have proved true over the years. Astronomers try to **investigate** the theory all the time. One way they do this is to use a "spectroscope." A spectroscope measures the color of light coming from an object. Changes in the color indicate whether an object is moving away from or toward the Earth.

Because of spectroscope readings scientists believe that the universe is still growing outward in every direction.

LEARN MORE! READ THESE ARTICLES...
GALAXIES • SOLAR SYSTEM • STARS

DID YOU KNOW?

Scientists believe that much of the universe may be made of something called "dark matter." This hidden mass may be a substance that human beings have never before encountered.

Answer: Everything in the universe is moving away from everything else. You can see how this works if you put black dots on a balloon, blow it up, and watch the dots spread apart.

The Invisible Magnet

Raise your arm. Keep it in that position for as long as you can. What happens?

After some time, your arm begins to hurt. Something seems to be pulling it down. Soon enough, you have to lower your arm.

It's a force called "gravity" that causes you to lower your arm. Gravity acts something like a magnet, tugging away at your arm as if it were a piece of metal.

We can't see gravity or touch it. We can only feel it. The Earth has gravity that pulls down on everything on or near it. It is this force that keeps us all on Earth.

The Moon and the Sun also have gravity. All bodies in the universe have gravity. In fact, gravity helps hold all of them together. Sir Isaac Newton first introduced the idea of gravity, and Albert Einstein added to Newton's ideas.

Gravity works in a two-way system. This means that all bodies have a pull on each other. For example, Earth's gravity forces the Moon to circle around it all the time. In return, the Moon's gravity attracts the waters of Earth's oceans to cause tides.

The force of gravity becomes weaker and weaker as we move away from its source. That is partly why astronauts can float around in outer space. They are too far away for the Earth to have much pull on them.

What do you think would happen if there were no gravity on Earth?

LEARN MORE! READ THESE ARTICLES…
ALBERT EINSTEIN • MOON • SIR ISAAC NEWTON

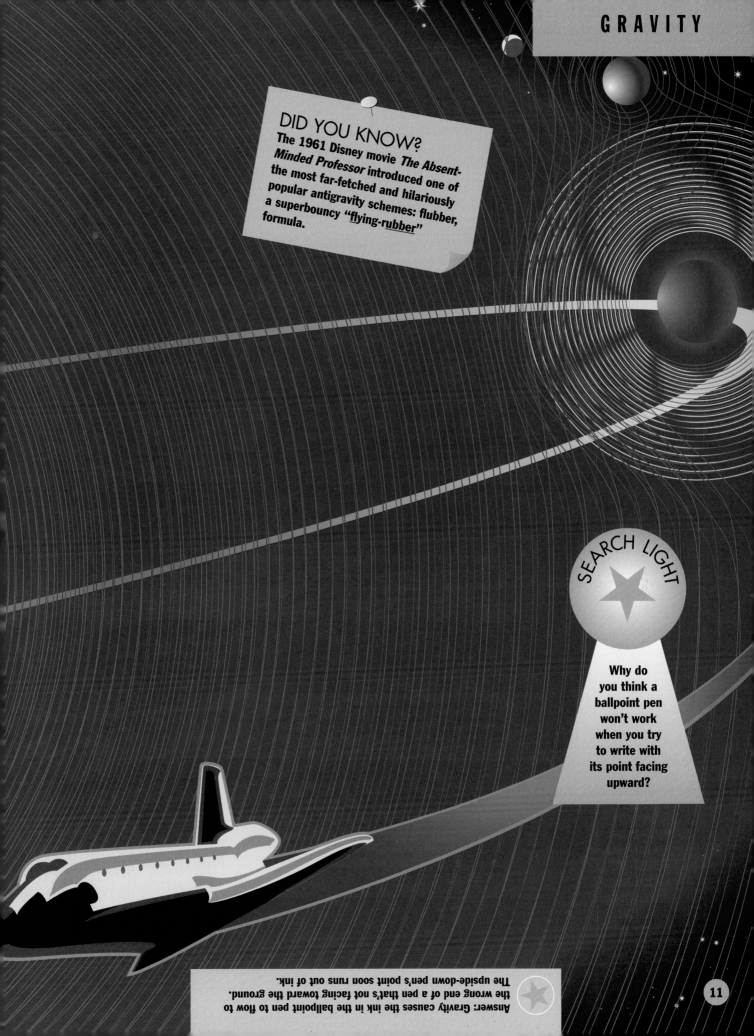

DID YOU KNOW?

The 1961 Disney movie *The Absent-Minded Professor* introduced one of the most far-fetched and hilariously popular antigravity schemes: flubber, a superbouncy "flying-rubber" formula.

SEARCH LIGHT

Why do you think a ballpoint pen won't work when you try to write with its point facing upward?

Answer: Gravity causes the ink in the ballpoint pen to flow to the wrong end of a pen that's not facing toward the ground. The upside-down pen's point soon runs out of ink.

Star Clusters

When we look at the sky at night, we may see thousands of stars shining brightly. They look as if they are just scattered around the sky. But actually, most stars are clustered together in huge groups. These groups are called "galaxies."

Our Sun is part of a galaxy. It is the Milky Way Galaxy. On a very clear night, if you look carefully at the sky, you might see part of this whitish band of stars stretching from one side to the other.

The universe is so huge that the Milky Way Galaxy is only one of many. Astronomers think that there are billions of galaxies in the universe. Each of these galaxies may contain trillions of stars, many much bigger than our own Sun! The Milky Way itself contains several billion stars.

Some galaxies have no regular shape. Others, like the Milky Way, are shaped somewhat like giant merry-go-rounds. Each has a center around which stars move in circles.

It is hard to see the other galaxies in the sky with the naked eye. Even though they are incredibly large, they are also incredibly far away. Scientists must use powerful telescopes to study other galaxies. For this reason it takes a long time to learn even a little bit about another galaxy. And there's still a great deal we haven't learned about our own galaxy.

LEARN MORE! READ THESE ARTICLES...
SOLAR SYSTEM • STARS • UNIVERSE

SEARCH LIGHT

Find and correct the error in the following sentence: There are many, many universes in the galaxy.

DID YOU KNOW?

Constellations, unlike galaxies, are groups of stars that people imagined as connecting to make pictures in the night sky. Named mostly for animals and mythological figures, constellations still help astronomers and navigators locate certain stars.

Our galaxy, the Milky Way, is shaped somewhat like a giant merry-go-round. Its billions of stars move in circles around a center.
© Myron Jay Dorf/Corbis

Answer: There are many, many galaxies in the universe.

Distant Fire

All stars are basically enormous balls of fire. They are made up of gases that give off both heat and light as they burn. Their power comes from nuclear energy, the same source that both powers atomic bombs and produces electricity in many parts of the world.

The life of a star spans billions of years. A star is born from clouds of dust and the **element** hydrogen. This cloud mass forms a spinning ball and becomes extremely hot. It becomes so hot that the hydrogen gas begins to glow. The glowing gas ball is called a "protostar" ("proto" means "beginning" or "first").

A protostar slowly becomes bigger until eventually it stops growing. It is then a star, and it can continue to glow for millions of years. But finally it starts to cool off. It turns red and grows larger once more. It becomes a "red giant." Then the star begins to die. How long a star lives depends on how big it is. The bigger the star, the longer it lives.

In large stars the heat inside the star produces iron. This iron acts like a sponge and soaks up the star's energy. The energy eventually causes a big explosion called a "supernova." In some cases, what is left may become a black hole. Black holes are like giant vacuum cleaners in space that suck up everything around them, including light.

Our Sun is still a young star, though it is already billions of years old. It will be many more billions of years before it begins to die. So there's still time to finish your homework.

LEARN MORE! READ THESE ARTICLES...
SUBRAHMANYAN CHANDRASEKHAR · GALAXIES · UNIVERSE

DID YOU KNOW?

After our own Sun, the nearest star to Earth is Alpha Proxima Centuri. It is 4.3 light-years away, or almost 800 million miles from Earth.

SEARCH LIGHT

True or false? Black holes were once stars.

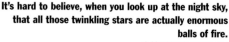

It's hard to believe, when you look up at the night sky, that all those twinkling stars are actually enormous balls of fire.
© Matthias Kulka/Corbis

Answer: TRUE. Black holes are former stars that have collapsed inward and now swallow up all material and light around them.

Wanderers
in the Sky

Billions of years ago there was a gigantic swirling cloud of gas and dust. This cloud packed together and became extremely hot. Eventually, the center of the cloud formed our Sun. The rest of the cloud clumped together until it formed the planets.

Nine planets in our solar system revolve (circle) around our Sun. Beginning with the one closest to the Sun, they are Mercury, Venus, Earth, Mars, Jupiter, Saturn, Uranus, Neptune, and Pluto.

The planets have been divided into two basic groups. There are Earth-like planets and Jupiter-like planets.

Earth-like planets are close to the Sun and made up of rock and metal. These planets are Mercury, Venus, Earth, and Mars. The other planets are larger and farther away from the Sun. These planets are Jupiter, Saturn, Uranus, and Neptune. These four planets have no solid surfaces. They are made up of gases and liquids.

But that's only eight planets. Pluto, farthest from the Sun, is neither Earth-like nor Jupiter-like. It is a frozen planet, the only one.

Each planet **rotates** on its **axis**. An axis is like an imaginary stick going through a planet's center from one end to the other. The planet spins just as if a giant hand had given this stick a mighty twist.

Most planets rotate from west to east. Only Venus, Uranus, and Pluto rotate from east to west. On these three planets the Sun seems to rise in the west and set in the east.

LEARN MORE! READ THESE ARTICLES...
ASTEROIDS • SOLAR SYSTEM • STARS

DID YOU KNOW?
Scientists have found three planets orbiting the star Upsilon Andromedae, a star much like our Sun. Some think this means there could be life on one of the planets.

SEARCH LIGHT

Group the
nine planets
according to
whether they're
made of *Gas, Ice,*
or *Rock/Metal.*

Jupiter - Saturn - Mars
- Venus - Uranus
- Pluto - Earth -
Mercury - Neptune

Answer: *Gas:* Jupiter, Saturn, Uranus, Neptune
Ice: Pluto
Rock/Metal: Mars, Venus, Earth, Mercury

17

Minor Planets

On January 1, 1801, a man named Giuseppe Piazzi found a new object in the sky. It was circling the Sun out beyond the planet Mars, and Piazzi thought it might be a comet. Some people thought that it was a new planet. Over the next few years many more objects were seen. All of these were much smaller than a planet. Astronomers now call these objects "asteroids," or minor planets.

There are thousands of asteroids in our solar system. They tend to vary in shape, ranging from large **spheres** to smaller slabs and potato-shaped objects. Some asteroids are big. Most are the size of a boulder. The asteroid that Piazzi found, called Ceres, is the biggest discovered so far. Its **diameter** is about 440 miles. Smaller asteroids form when two big asteroids smash into each other and break up. Astronomers think that there are millions of tiny asteroids in the solar system.

Like planets, all asteroids in our solar system circle the Sun. The path that a planet or an asteroid follows when it circles the Sun is called an "orbit." Most asteroids are found farther from the Sun than Earth, between the orbits of Mars and Jupiter. Some, though, come quite close to the Sun.

Many people believe that millions of years ago an asteroid hit Earth and led to the dinosaurs' dying out. Some filmmakers in Hollywood have even made popular films, such as *Armageddon*, using the idea of an asteroid hitting Earth.

LEARN MORE! READ THESE ARTICLES...
COMETS · PLANETS · SOLAR SYSTEM

SEARCH LIGHT

Fill in the blank: An asteroid might have been involved in the disappearance of the dinosaurs when it crashed into _____.

DID YOU KNOW?

Here's a surprise: not all asteroids are in outer space! Starfish are also called asteroids. The name that these two very different things share means "starlike."

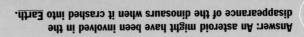

Answer: An asteroid might have been involved in the disappearance of the dinosaurs when it crashed into Earth.

SEARCH LIGHT

If Halley's Comet came around in 1759, 1835, 1910, and 1986, about how many years does it take to appear?

DID YOU KNOW?

American author Mark Twain was born in 1835 on a day when Halley's Comet could be seen in the sky. Just as he predicted, he died when Halley's Comet was again seen in the sky, in 1910.

Rocketing Masses
with Fuzzy Tails

The word "comet" comes from a Greek word that means "hairy one." A comet sometimes looks like a star with a hairy tail. But a comet is not a star. Like the Moon, a comet has no light of its own. A comet shines from the sunlight bouncing off it. Like the Earth, a comet goes around the Sun, so it may appear again and again.

But if a comet isn't a star, what is it?

Some scientists think that a large part of a comet is ice. The rest is bits of iron and dust and perhaps a few big chunks of rock. When sunshine melts the ice in a comet, great clouds of gas go streaming behind it. These clouds make the bright fuzzy-looking tail.

Long ago when there were no streetlights and the air was very clean, everyone could see the comets. Unlike the stars that shone every night, comets seemed to appear quite suddenly. So people thought that they would bring bad luck such as floods, hungry times, or sickness.

Edmond Halley, who lived over 200 years ago, discovered about 24 different comets. One that keeps coming back was named for him because he figured out when it would return. Halley first saw it in 1759, and it reappeared in 1835, 1910, and 1986. The next time it comes near the Earth will be in the year 2060.

How old will you be then?

LEARN MORE! READ THESE ARTICLES…
ASTEROIDS • ASTRONOMY • SOLAR SYSTEM

Derke/O'Hara/Stone

Answer: Halley's Comet generally comes around every 76 years, though sometimes it takes just 75.

SEARCH LIGHT

Which of
these would
you *not* find in
the solar system?
- galaxy
- star
- planet
- comet
- asteroid

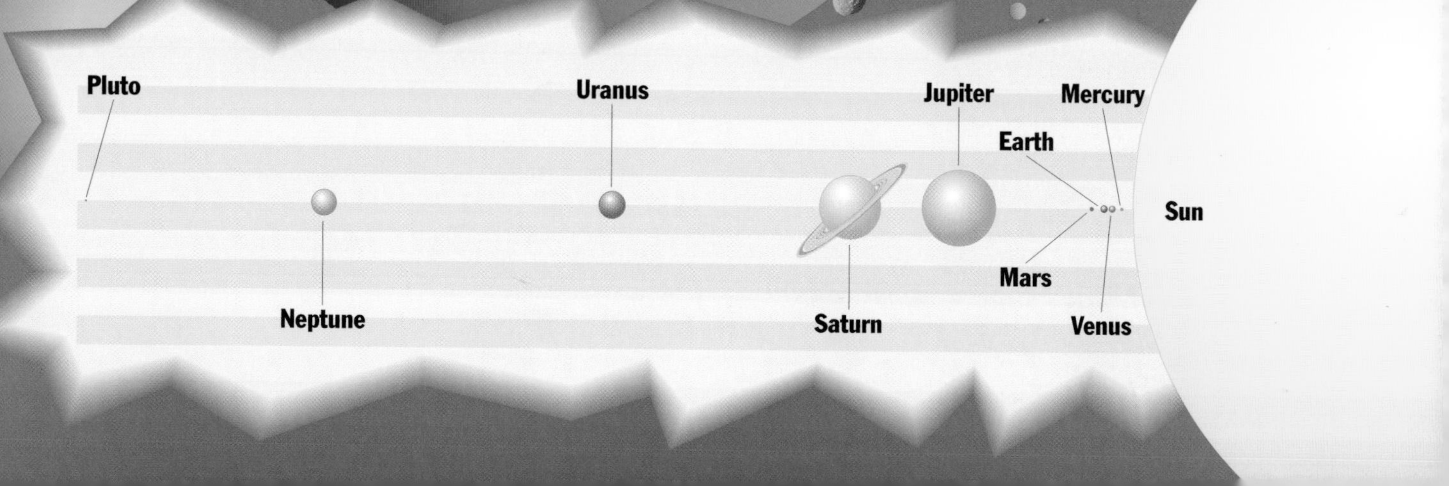

Pluto

Uranus

Jupiter

Mercury

Earth

Sun

Neptune

Saturn

Mars

Venus

Family of the Sun

Imagine a huge black space. The Sun moves through this vast space, bringing many smaller bodies with it. These bodies include planets, asteroids, comets, meteors, and tiny **molecules** of gases. The Sun and its companions are known as a "solar system." Many solar systems and stars clustered together make up galaxies.

Astronomers do not know how far out our solar system extends. We think that Pluto is the last planet to **orbit** the Sun, but there could still be more. At its farthest point from the Sun, Pluto is about 4.5 billion miles away.

The Sun provides energy for the rest of the solar system. It also provides the heat and light necessary for life on our planet. And its **gravity** keeps the planets, comets, and other bodies in orbit.

The planets are the largest and most **massive** members of the solar system after the Sun. There are nine known planets: Mercury, Venus, Earth, Mars, Jupiter, Saturn, Uranus, Neptune, and Pluto.

Asteroids, known as "minor planets," are smaller bodies. Most asteroids lie between Mars and Jupiter. Ceres is the largest asteroid.

A comet appears in the sky as a fuzzy spot of light with a tail streaming away from it. It is made up of dust and frozen gases. As this giant dirty snowball moves closer to the Sun, the ice melts and makes what looks like a tail. Halley's Comet is probably the most famous of all.

LEARN MORE! READ THESE ARTICLES…
ASTEROIDS • GALAXIES • PLANETS

DID YOU KNOW?
The Sun's temperature on the surface is about 10,000°-11,000° F. That's 100 times hotter than a really hot day on Earth!

Answer: Galaxies are made up of stars and solar systems, not the other way around.

The Planet Nearest to the Sun

SEARCH LIGHT

Why would being closest to the Sun make Mercury hard to study? (Hint: Think of two important things the Sun gives us.)

Mercury is the first of our nine planets, the closest to the Sun. Because it seems to move so quickly across the night sky, it was named for the wing-footed Roman god. Mercury is visible to the naked eye from Earth, just before dawn and just after sundown.

Mercury is only slightly bigger than Earth's Moon. Its entire surface is airless, though many different gases surround the planet. Mercury is also a place of extreme temperatures. Its hottest temperature is 755° F and its coldest is −280° F.

In 1974 and 1975 the spacecraft Mariner 10 flew as close to Mercury as possible, sending back pictures and other information. Scientists found the planet's surface covered with a layer of broken rock called "regolith." Mercury also has large ice patches at its north pole.

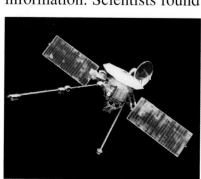

Mariner 10 space probe, which sent valuable pictures of and other data about Mercury.
© Corbis

Some regions of Mercury are covered with heavy **craters**, probably created when the planet ran into other bodies as it was forming. Other regions show gently rolling plains. These may have been smoothed by volcanic lava flow. The planet also features long steep cliffs called "scarps" in some areas.

Mercury takes 88 Earth days to go around the Sun once, which gives it a very short year. But it takes 1,416 hours to complete one **rotation** about its **axis**, so it has a very long day.

Mercury has a sunrise only once in every two of its years. This is because, after one of its very long days, the Sun is in a different place in Mercury's sky. It takes three of Mercury's days (about 176 of our days) for the Sun to once again rise in the morning sky.

LEARN MORE! READ THESE ARTICLES...
PLANETS • PLUTO • SOLAR SYSTEM

DID YOU KNOW?
It's no wonder that Mercury was named after the speedy messenger of the gods. The planet travels at an incredible 30 miles per second.

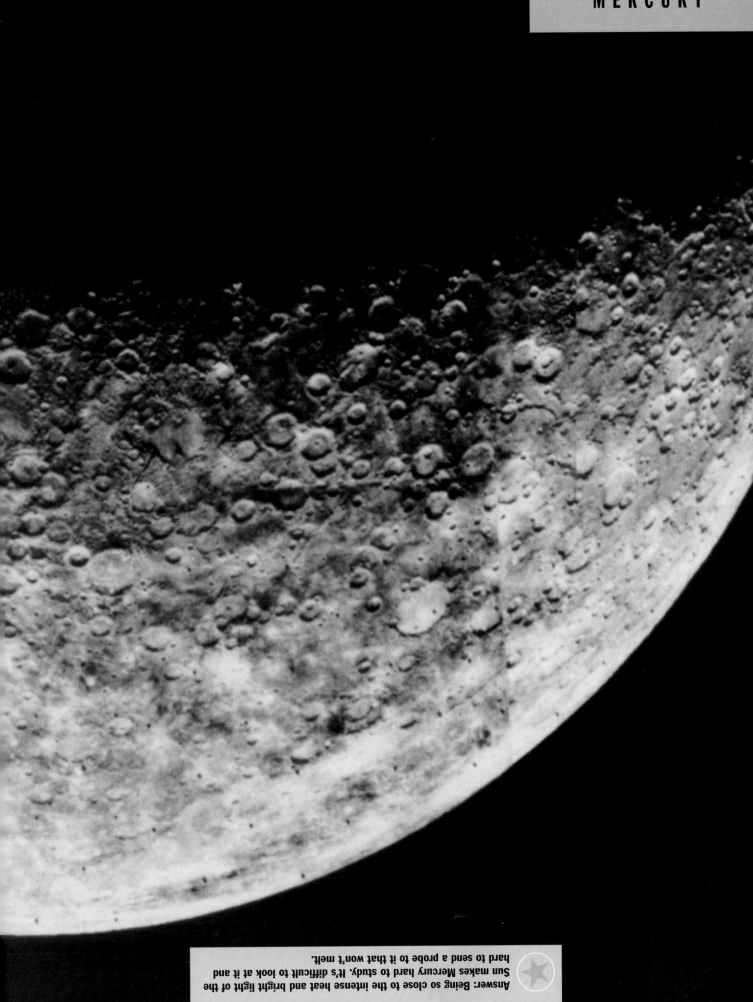

Answer: Being so close to the intense heat and bright light of the Sun makes Mercury hard to study. It's difficult to look at it and hard to send a probe to it that won't melt.

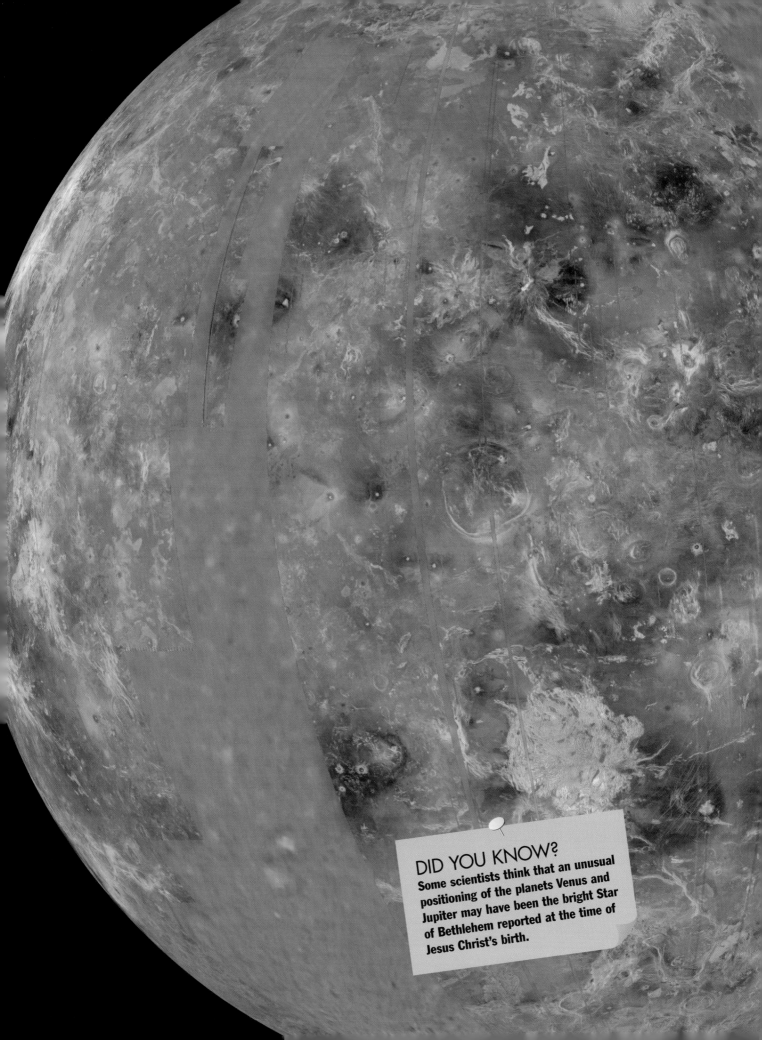

DID YOU KNOW?

Some scientists think that an unusual positioning of the planets Venus and Jupiter may have been the bright Star of Bethlehem reported at the time of Jesus Christ's birth.

A Morning and Evening Star

Venus is the second planet from the Sun. It is named for the Roman goddess of love and beauty, perhaps because it shines so brightly. It sometimes appears brilliantly in the western sky as the "evening star"

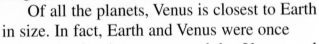

and brightly in the predawn eastern sky as the "morning star."

Although Venus is the planet closest to Earth, it is difficult to study because it is completely covered by thick layers of clouds. Venus' dense cloud layers do not allow much sunlight to reach the planet's surface. They do, however, help keep the surface very hot. So do the planet's active volcanoes. The temperature on the Venusian surface reaches about 860° F. The highest clouds, by contrast, have a daily range of 77° to −236° F.

Of all the planets, Venus is closest to Earth in size. In fact, Earth and Venus were once regarded as sister planets. Some scientists have suggested that Venus could support some form of life, perhaps in its clouds. Humans, however, could not breathe the air there.

Several spacecraft have visited and sent back information about Venus, beginning with Mariner 2 in 1962. The immensely powerful Hubble Space Telescope has also provided considerable **data** about the planet.

Scientists have learned that the surface of Venus is marked with hundreds of large meteor **craters**. These craters suggest that since it formed, the surface of Venus has changed in a different way from Earth's surface. Earth has only a few large craters that are easy to recognize.

Venus is different from Earth in another way, too. It hasn't got a moon.

Magellan space probe being launched by the space shuttle *Atlantis* in 1989.
© NASA/Roger Ressmeyer/Corbis

SEARCH LIGHT

How are Venus and Earth alike? What makes them different?

LEARN MORE! READ THESE ARTICLES…
MARS • PLANETS • SOLAR SYSTEM

Answer: Earth and Venus are roughly the same size, and both planets have active volcanoes. Venus too might be able to support some form of life, though probably in its clouds. But Earth is different in having water, a moon, and breathable air.

SEARCH LIGHT

Find out what you would weigh on the Moon. Take your weight and divide by 7.

A Trip to the Moon

Would you like to go to the Moon? Someday you may be able to. Astronauts have already visited the Moon. They brought their own food, water, and air. You would have to bring these things along too, because the Moon doesn't have them.

Astronaut Edwin E. ("Buzz") Aldrin on July 20, 1969, one of the first two humans to walk on the Moon.
NASA/JPL/Caltech

Compared with the planets, the Moon is very near to the Earth. It is only 239,000 miles away. Spaceships travel fast enough to cover that distance in a matter of hours.

Someday there may be little towns on the Moon. The first ones will probably be covered over and filled with air. When you're inside the Moon town, you'll be able to breathe normally without a space suit or air tanks. But you will need a space suit and an air tank to go outside.

Once you walk outside the Moon town, you will feel a lot lighter. You will be able to take giant steps of more than ten feet. You'll be able to throw a baseball almost out of sight. This is because the Moon has fairly weak gravity, the force that keeps things from flying off into space.

Gravity is also what gives your body weight. You would not weigh as much on the Moon as you do on the Earth. If you weigh 40 pounds on the Earth, you would weigh only 6 pounds on the Moon!

From the Moon you'll see many more stars than you can see from the Earth. They'll also seem much brighter, because you won't be looking through layers of air and pollution. And you'll be able to enjoy this view for two whole weeks at a time. That's the length of the Moon's night!

LEARN MORE! READ THESE ARTICLES…
ASTRONAUTS • GRAVITY • SPACECRAFT

Answer: If your Earth weight is 56 pounds, for example, your Moon weight would be only about 8 pounds.

DID YOU KNOW?
The reason Mars appears red is that the planet's soil contains a lot of rusted iron.

The Red Planet

Mars is the fourth planet from the Sun. It is named after the ancient Roman god of war. Since the planet is red in color, it also called the "red planet."

The first spacecraft to fly close to Mars was Mariner 4, in 1965. In the 1970s two Viking spacecraft landed there, and in July 1997 Mars Pathfinder set down. These efforts sent back from Mars soil sample reports, pictures, and other **data**—but no proof of life.

Because of similarities between Mars and Earth, however, scientists think there could be some form of life on Mars.

Mars is half the size of Earth. Its thin air is made up mainly of carbon dioxide and other gases, so we wouldn't be able to breathe it. And the Martian surface is much colder than Earth's would be

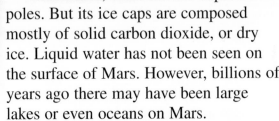

Martian surface of rocks and fine-grained material, photographed in 1976 by the Viking 1 spacecraft.
NASA

at that distance from the Sun. Two small moons, Phobos and Deimos, **orbit** Mars.

Like Earth, Mars has ice caps at both poles. But its ice caps are composed mostly of solid carbon dioxide, or dry ice. Liquid water has not been seen on the surface of Mars. However, billions of years ago there may have been large lakes or even oceans on Mars.

Also like Earth, Mars has different seasons. Mars takes 687 Earth days to go around the Sun once. This means its year is almost twice as long as ours. But since it spins on its **axis** once every 24 hours and 37 minutes, its day is just about the same.

Despite being small, Mars has the largest volcano in our solar system, Olympus Mons. It stands about three times higher than Earth's highest point, Mount Everest, and covers an area just a bit smaller than the entire country of Poland.

LEARN MORE! READ THESE ARTICLES…
EXTRATERRESTRIAL LIFE • SOLAR SYSTEM • SPACECRAFT

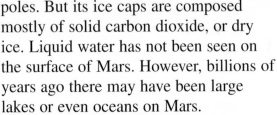

SEARCH LIGHT

What surface feature of Mars holds a record?

In this image taken by the Hubble Space Telescope in 1997, you can see the north polar ice cap (white area) at the top and some huge volcanoes (the darker red spots) in the left half of the photo.
Phil James (Univ. Toledo), Todd Clancy (Space Science Inst., Boulder, CO), Steve Lee (Univ. Colorado), and NASA

Answer: Mars has the largest volcano in our solar system.

King of the Planets

Jupiter is the biggest planet in our solar system. It is so big that all the other eight planets could fit inside it at the same time and there would still be room left over. The planet is named after the king of the Roman gods.

Jupiter is a giant ball of gases, mostly the **elements** hydrogen and helium. Helium is the gas that makes balloons float in air, and hydrogen is

Jupiter's Great Red Spot (colors boosted) as seen by Voyager I spacecraft, 1979.
Jet Propulsion Laboratory/NASA

one part of water. The center of the planet is probably made of a hot liquid, like a thick soup.

Jupiter isn't a very welcoming place. It is extremely hot. It is thousands of times hotter than the hottest place on Earth.

Also, storms rage on Jupiter's surface almost all the time. Scientists have seen one storm there that is almost twice as wide as the Earth! It is called the Great Red Spot. It has been raging on Jupiter's surface for at least a few hundred years.

Jupiter definitely has over 50 moons, and probably more. Some of them are much bigger than Earth's Moon. One is even bigger than the planet Mercury! Others are tiny, only a few miles across.

Astronomers have found something very exciting on one of Jupiter's moons, called Europa. They believe that it has a huge ocean of water below its surface that may have simple life forms in it.

LEARN MORE! READ THESE ARTICLES...
PLANETS • SATURN • SOLAR SYSTEM

SEARCH LIGHT

Find and correct the error in this sentence: A storm known as the Big Red Dog has been raging on Jupiter's surface for hundreds of years.

DID YOU KNOW?
Jupiter has more than 50 known moons, and Earth has only 1. But that seems fair, since Jupiter is 1,500 times bigger than Earth!

The Ringed Planet

Saturn is the sixth planet from the Sun. It is named after the god of **agriculture** in Roman mythology. Saturn is easily visible through a small telescope, and its famous spectacular rings are quite clear. The astronomer Galileo was the first to see the rings through his telescope.

Saturn is a gas planet, like Jupiter, Neptune, and Uranus. Very little of it is solid. Most of Saturn consists of the **elements** hydrogen and helium. It is covered with bands of colored clouds and surrounded by a number of thin rings made of water ice and ice-covered **particles**. Cameras on the Voyager 1 and 2 spacecraft showed that these rings range in size from a speck of dust to the size of a house. Voyager 2 took the picture you see here.

Because Saturn is made of different substances, different parts of the planet **rotate** at different rates. The upper atmosphere swirls around the planet at rates between 10 hours and 10 minutes (Earth time) and about 10 hours and 40 minutes. The inner core, which is probably made of hot rocks, rotates in about 10 hours and 39 minutes.

But Saturn takes 29 years and 5 months in Earth time to go around the Sun just once. The Earth goes around the Sun once every 365 days. Saturn's year is so much longer because the planet is so much farther away from the Sun.

Astronomers have found that at least 30 moons **orbit** Saturn. The largest of these is Titan, which is almost as large as the planets Mercury or Mars. In our photograph, you can see two moons as tiny white spots to the lower left of (Dione) and below (Rhea) the planet. Other satellites include Mimas, Enceladus, and Tethys.

SEARCH LIGHT

Saturn's many rings are made of
a) ice.
b) dust.
c) gas.
d) rock.

DID YOU KNOW?
Saturn is more than ten times the size of the Earth. But the planet is so light that it could float on an ocean of water.

LEARN MORE! READ THESE ARTICLES...
JUPITER • PLANETS • SOLAR SYSTEM

Answer: a) ice.

King George's Star

Uranus is the seventh planet from the Sun. Its name is that of the god of the heavens in ancient Greek mythology.

When William Herschel discovered this planet in March 1781, he named it Georgium Sidus (George's Star) in honor of his king, George III of England. Others called it Herschel. In about 1850 scientists began to use the name Uranus.

The spacecraft Voyager 2 visited Uranus some 200 years after Herschel discovered it. Findings confirmed that Uranus is a large gas planet. Small amounts of methane gas in its upper atmosphere give the planet a blue-green color.

It takes Uranus 84 of Earth's years to go around the Sun once, so its year is 84 times as long as ours. But the planet takes only about 17 hours to spin on its **axis** once, so its day is shorter.

Unlike other planets, Uranus lies on its side at an odd angle. It points first one pole toward the Sun, then its equator, and then the other pole. So it is not yet clear which is the planet's "north" pole.

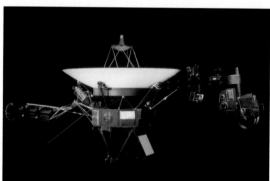

Voyager 2, the spacecraft that reported Uranus' makeup.
© Corbis

As with other gas planets, such as Jupiter, Saturn, and Neptune, Uranus has a system of rings. In some places the rings are so thin that they seem to disappear.

The planet has 20 known moons that are made mostly of ice and are heavily **cratered**. The five major ones are Miranda, Ariel, Umbriel, Titania, and Oberon. Their names are those of characters from works by William Shakespeare and Alexander Pope.

LEARN MORE! READ THESE ARTICLES...
PLANETS • SATURN • SOLAR SYSTEM

SEARCH LIGHT

Find and correct the error in the following sentence: When William Herschel discovered Uranus in 1781, he named it Georgium Sidus for his dog.

DID YOU KNOW?

Between Uranus and Saturn lies Chiron, an object first considered an asteroid, then reclassified as a comet. Its name reflects its confused identity: Chiron was a centaur, a half man and half horse in Greek mythology.

Answer: When William Herschel discovered Uranus in 1781, he named it Georgium Sidus for his king.

The Eighth Planet

Neptune is the eighth planet from the Sun. It is named after the Roman god of the sea.

The planet Neptune was discovered in 1846, but little was known about it until the spacecraft Voyager 2 visited it in August 1989.

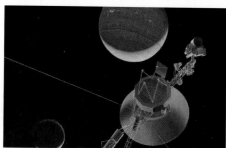

Artist's idea of Voyager 2 leaving Neptune after it visited that planet (seen in the background).
© Corbis

Neptune is made up mostly of gases. Its bluish color comes from its thick atmosphere of hydrogen, helium, and methane. Like other gas planets, such as Jupiter and Saturn, Neptune has rapid winds and big storms. The winds on Neptune are the fastest known in our solar system, reaching speeds of about 1,250 miles per hour.

The planet rotates quickly, once every 16.1 hours. This means its day is about two-thirds as long as ours. But it has a much longer year. There are about 60,225 days in one Neptune year. That's how many days it takes the planet to **orbit** the Sun. It has been in the same year since its discovery in 1846. Each season on Neptune lasts for 41 years.

Like Saturn, Neptune has rings, but they aren't as noticeable. Neptune also has 11 known moons. Triton is the largest moon. Triton is slowly drawing closer to Neptune. It is believed that it will someday crash into the planet.

LEARN MORE! READ THESE ARTICLES...
PLANETS • SATURN • SOLAR SYSTEM

DID YOU KNOW?

It's more than just a little chilly on Neptune. Its average temperature is –373° F. By comparison, Antarctica, the coldest place on Earth, has measured a mere –129° F at its coldest.

SEARCH LIGHT

Neptune has a shorter day than Earth. So why is Neptune's year so much longer than ours? (Hint: Neptune is the eighth planet from the Sun, and Earth is only the third.)

NASA

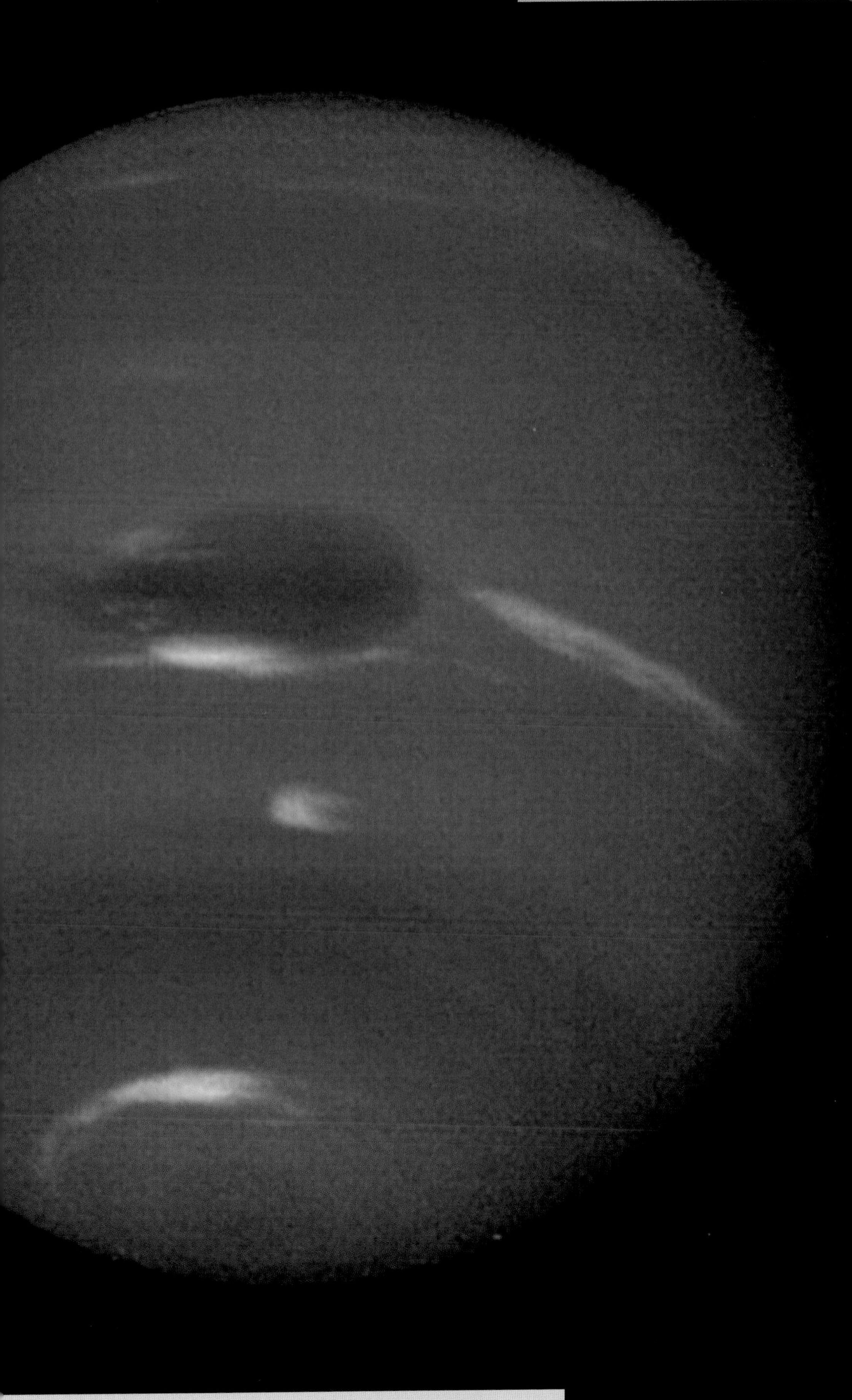

Answer: Neptune is so much farther from the Sun than Earth that it takes the eighth planet about 165 times as long to orbit the Sun.

SEARCH LIGHT

Fill in the
blanks:
Pluto is so
_____
that it wasn't
discovered until
_____.

The Lonely Planet

In Roman mythology Pluto was the god of the underworld. Pluto is the name given to another dark mystery: the smallest planet in our solar system. Planet Pluto is smaller than the Earth's Moon and is the farthest planet from the Sun—most of the time.

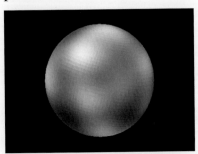

One of the first photos of Pluto's surface, taken with the Hubble Space Telescope.
Alan Stern (Southwestern Research Institute), Marc Bule (Lowell Observatory), NASA, and the European Space Agency

Every 248 years Pluto's odd **orbit** takes it closer to the Sun than the planet Neptune goes. For 20 years Neptune becomes the farthest planet, as happened from 1979 to 1999.

Pluto is so distant and small that it wasn't discovered until 1930. It is the only planet that hasn't been visited by a spacecraft. Only recently have very strong instruments like the Hubble Space Telescope given us some details about the mysterious faraway planet.

Tiny Pluto is only about 1,485 miles across from pole to pole. It's not entirely clear what the planet is made of, but scientists think it may be 50 to 75 percent rock and the rest frozen water and gases. So far from the Sun's warmth, all of Pluto is permanently frozen. Because of its small size and icy makeup and because it travels in a part of the solar system where some comets are thought to come from, scientists wonder if Pluto is really more like a giant comet than a planet.

Pluto spins in the opposite direction from most of the other planets. If you were on the planet, you would see the Sun rise in the west and set in the east. A day on Pluto is equal to six days and 25 minutes on Earth. Pluto's year takes more than 90,155 of our days.

Pluto's moon, Charon, wasn't discovered until 1978. As you can see from the large photo, Charon is about half the size of Pluto—quite large for a moon. In fact, some scientists consider Pluto and Charon to be a double planet.

LEARN MORE! READ THESE ARTICLES...
NEPTUNE • SOLAR SYSTEM • SPACECRAFT

DID YOU KNOW?
Walt Disney's dog character Pluto was named for the ninth planet. Pluto the dog first appeared in 1930, the same year the planet Pluto was discovered.

Answer: Pluto is so distant that it wasn't discovered until 1930.

Ancient Mathematician-Astronomer

More than 1,500 years ago the Indian scientist Aryabhata came up with some rules and ideas in mathematics that we still use today, as well as some important facts about astronomy.

Aryabhata wrote *Aryabhatiya*, his major work, when he was only 23 years old. Part of the book discusses two kinds of mathematics: geometry (a kind of math for measuring shapes and objects) and algebra (which solves some number problems).

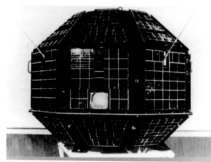

Aryabhata, India's first unmanned satellite.
Indian Space Research Organization

The rest of the *Aryabhatiya* talks about the planets, the stars, and space. Aryabhata was the first astronomer to state that the Earth is round and **rotates** on its **axis**. He explained that the Sun and the night sky only seem to move across the sky from east to west each day because the Earth rotates the other direction, from west to east.

Fill in the blank: Aryabhata figured out how long the _____ is without using a clock.

Aryabhata figured out that one Earth rotation lasts 23 hours, 56 minutes, and 4 1/10 seconds. That is, he figured out how long one day is. Today's exact measurement is only a tiny fraction different! Of course, to simplify things we count our day as having 24 hours.

Aryabhata also explained events called "**eclipses**," which happen when the Sun or the Moon goes dark. Hindu mythology says eclipses occur when Rahu, a planet, gobbles up the Sun or Moon. But Aryabhata realized that eclipses happen because of shadows cast by the Earth or the Moon on one another.

The Indian government honored this great scientist in 1975 by naming the country's first satellite after him.

LEARN MORE! READ THESE ARTICLES...
ASTRONOMY • SUBRAHMANYAN CHANDRASEKHAR • NICOLAUS COPERNICUS

These are the ruins of Nalanda, the ancient Buddhist learning center where Aryabhata studied and worked. Khagola, the observatory at Nalanda, gave its name to the term in India for astronomy: *khagola-shastra*.
© Lindsay Hebberd/Corbis

DID YOU KNOW?

Like many ancient scientific works, Aryabhata's great book, *Aryabhatiya*, was written in verses as a kind of poetry.

Answer: Aryabhata figured out how long the day is without using a clock.

SEARCH LIGHT

Find and correct the error in the following sentence: Copernicus studied the skies and finally decided that the Sun circles the Earth.

Student of the Sky

Hundreds of years ago many people thought that the Earth stayed still and the Sun went around it. Then came a man named Nicolaus Copernicus, who said that it was the Sun that stayed still and the Earth that moved. And he was mostly right.

Copernicus was born on February 19, 1473, in Poland. His father died a few years after Copernicus was born, and a wealthy uncle brought the young boy up. He sent him to the University of Kraków to study mathematics. There Copernicus also studied the stars and planets.

Copernicus didn't believe that the Earth was the center of the universe and that all the other planets and stars circled around it. He studied the sky

An image of the solar system as Copernicus imagined it.
© Stefano Bianchetti/Corbis

for years and finally decided that the Sun sat at the center of the universe. The Earth and the other planets spun around the Sun.

Some of what Copernicus said wasn't correct. We know today that all the planets and the stars, including the Sun, move constantly. We also know that the Sun is the center not of the universe but rather of the solar system. Yet Copernicus was right in some ways. It is true that the Earth circles the Sun.

Copernicus presented his ideas in a book called *On the Revolutions of the Celestial Spheres*. The book wasn't published for 13 years because the Roman Catholic church opposed it. It is said that Copernicus received the first copy as he was dying, on May 24, 1543.

LEARN MORE! READ THESE ARTICLES...
ASTRONOMY • JOHANNES KEPLER • SOLAR SYSTEM

Unlike most people in his day, Nicolaus Copernicus didn't believe that the Earth was the center of the universe. And his studies eventually showed that he was right.
© Bettmann/Corbis

Answer: Copernicus studied the skies and finally decided that the Earth circles the Sun.

DID YOU KNOW?
Kepler's grave was lost during a war, but the words he composed for his gravestone survive:
I used to measure the heavens,
now I shall measure the shadows of the earth.
Although my soul was from heaven,
the shadow of my body lies here.

Stargazer

Johannes Kepler was born on December 27, 1571, in Germany. He was to grow up to be an important astronomer who made many discoveries by studying the stars. Astronomers study the movements of planets, stars, comets, and meteors. However, for most of his life Kepler studied and taught mathematics.

When he was 23 years old, Kepler became an official calendar maker. Calendar making was a difficult job because certain church holy days

Diagram of Kepler's first model of the universe.
© Bettmann/Corbis

had to happen just as a particular star was in a particular spot in the sky. It took a lot of complicated math to make a calendar come out right.

In 1597 Kepler published his first important work, *The Cosmographic Mystery*. Kepler's book explained the distance of the planets from the Sun. Kepler also said that all the planets revolve around the Sun and that the Sun remains in one position—an idea that built on those of the earlier astronomer Nicolaus Copernicus.

In 1600 Kepler moved to Prague, where he soon became Emperor Rudolf II's **imperial** mathematician, the most important mathematics post in Europe. Kepler discovered that Mars's orbit is an ellipse (an oval-like shape) rather than a circle. He also gave important laws for the motion of all of the planets around the Sun.

Kepler's scientific work was focused on astronomy. But he also studied other sciences and mathematics so he could learn everything possible about the stars.

LEARN MORE! READ THESE ARTICLES...
ARYABHATA • ASTRONOMY • NICOLAUS COPERNICUS

SEARCH LIGHT

Kepler was teacher of
a) science.
b) German.
c) math.
d) astronomy.

Johannes Kepler became the official mathematician to Emperor Rudolf II. This picture shows him explaining some of his discoveries to the emperor.
© Bettmann/Corbis

Answer: c) math.

DID YOU KNOW?
The story of Newton and the apple is a good one, but it is not true. Like George Washington and his cherry tree, the apple story is just a good way to remember something important about someone famous.

An Apple, an Idea

When you throw a ball into the air, do you wonder why it always comes back down? Why doesn't it keep going up?

One man did more than wonder. He was Sir Isaac Newton.

There is a story that as Newton sat under an apple tree, an apple struck him on the head. He wondered why the apple fell down instead of up. Was some force that no one could see pulling the apple to the ground?

Newton's reflecting telescope, made in 1668.
© James A. Sugar/Corbis

Actually, it was Newton's observation of the motions of the planets that contributed most importantly to his great discovery: the Law of Universal Gravitation. This "natural law" helps explain how the Earth and the Moon and the planets keep from bumping into each other. It explains why things feel light or heavy and what makes them fall to the ground.

What Newton decided was that everything has gravity. And every object's gravity has a pull on everything else around it. Heavy things pull harder than light ones.

Newton figured out many other things too. Did you know that white light is actually made of seven colors? They are the colors that make up a rainbow. Newton discovered that. He let the light pass through a **prism**, and the seven colors all came out separately. He then let the colors pass through another prism and they combined back into white light.

Newton's investigations also led him to invent the first reflecting telescope, which uses mirrors to gather light to improve a telescope's capability. His design is still used by amateur telescope makers.

Isaac Newton, one of the greatest scientists who ever lived, died in 1727 and was buried in Westminster Abbey in London, England. He was the first scientist to be honored this way.

LEARN MORE! READ THESE ARTICLES...
ALBERT EINSTEIN • GRAVITY • PLANETS

SEARCH LIGHT

Find and correct the error in the following sentence: Newton's theory of reflecting telescopes helped explain how the planets keep from bumping into each other.

Sir Isaac Newton's theory of gravity contributed to his lasting reputation as one of the greatest scientists of all time.
© Bettmann/Corbis

Answer: Newton's theory of gravitation (or gravity) helped explain how the planets keep from bumping into each other.

49

A Brilliant Wonderer

Young Albert Einstein didn't always do well in school. His teachers thought he took too long to answer questions. And often they got upset because Albert thought of questions they couldn't answer.

The Einstein Memorial, a sculpture honoring the great scientist, in Washington, D.C., U.S.
© Roman Soumar/Corbis

The more Albert learned, the more things he thought about. The more he thought, the more questions he had. By age 12 he had decided that he would solve the riddle of the "huge world," the universe.

Einstein thought there must be some rules to explain why everything in the universe, big and little, acts as it does. How can gravity attract distant objects through empty space? What makes tiny atoms stick together to form all the different things there are?

He thought and thought until he believed he had some of the answers for things that scientists had long tried to figure out, such as what makes gravity work and how fast light can travel. Einstein even proved such unexpected things as the fact that light bends under the force of gravity.

You may have heard of Einstein's famous formula $E = mc^2$. This stands for a complex idea called "relativity." But in the simplest terms it shows that a small **particle** of matter is equal to an enormous quantity of energy.

Einstein introduced entirely new ways of thinking about time, space, matter, energy, and gravity. His ideas guided such scientific advances as space exploration and the control of atomic energy. One of the concepts he explained, the **photoelectric effect**, led to something most people enjoy daily: television.

SEARCH LIGHT

Find and correct the error in the following sentence: Albert Einstein invented gravity.

LEARN MORE! READ THESE ARTICLES...
ARYABHATA • GRAVITY • UNIVERSE

DID YOU KNOW?
One story about Einstein has it that he once used a check for $1,500 as a bookmark—and lost it.

Albert Einstein, shown here in his study, introduced entirely new ways of thinking about time, space, matter, energy, and gravity.
© Bettmann/Corbis

Answer: Albert Einstein explained gravity.

DID YOU KNOW?
Some scientists think it might be possible to travel through black holes to other parts of the universe, assuming you could somehow survive the crushing gravity.

52

Discovering How Stars Grow

Astronomer Subrahmanyan Chandrasekhar was born in Lahore, India (now in Pakistan). He studied at home, then attended universities in India and England. He traveled to the United States to work and became a U.S. citizen in 1953.

Chandrasekhar's work on stars helped explain how the strange space **phenomena** called "black holes" are born.

Lalitha Chandrasekhar at the unveiling of the Chandra X-Ray Observatory, named to honor her husband.
© Reuters NewMedia Inc./Corbis

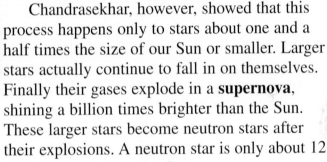

SEARCH LIGHT

True or false? Chandrasekhar is known for his work on the Sun.

By the early 1930s scientists had decided that over billions of years a star changes its chemical makeup and its energy drains away. The star then starts to shrink, pulled into a tight ball by its own **gravity**. It ends up about the size of the Earth and becomes a "white dwarf" star.

Chandrasekhar, however, showed that this process happens only to stars about one and a half times the size of our Sun or smaller. Larger stars actually continue to fall in on themselves. Finally their gases explode in a **supernova**, shining a billion times brighter than the Sun. These larger stars become neutron stars after their explosions. A neutron star is only about 12 miles across, but it has as much matter in it as the Sun.

Even bigger stars than those will collapse into black holes. Black holes have so much gravity in such a small amount of space that nothing can escape from them, not even light!

Chandrasekhar's discoveries were so important that they were named the "Chandrasekhar limit" for him. And in 1983 he was awarded the Nobel Prize for Physics for his contributions to scientific knowledge.

LEARN MORE! READ THESE ARTICLES...
ARYABHATA · GRAVITY · STARS

On the University of Chicago campus where he taught, Subrahmanyan Chandrasekhar sits at the base of a statue named "Nuclear Energy," created by sculptor Henry Moore.
© Bettmann/Corbis

Answer: FALSE. Chandrasekhar is known for his work on stars bigger than the Sun—stars that become black holes when they die.

First American Woman in Space

Sally Kristen Ride was the first American woman to fly into outer space. Only two other women had ever flown in space before, both from the former Soviet Union.

Ride did not grow up planning to be an astronaut. She actually started out as an athlete and was a talented tennis player. But she decided to go to college instead, studying first English and then science.

Ride was one of about a thousand women who applied to be an astronaut and serve as a scientist on the new space shuttle flights. While still finishing her **graduate school** education, Ride was chosen by NASA (the National Aeronautics and Space Administration) to be one of six new female astronauts.

In 1979 she completed her NASA training, earning her pilot's license at the same time. Four years later, on June 18, 1983, she became the first American woman in space. Ride was chosen as flight engineer aboard the space shuttle *Challenger*. Her work as a scientist meant that she could **monitor** and run the shuttle's complicated equipment.

Ride remembers that "the flight was the most fun I'll ever have in my life."

She flew into space a second time on October 13, 1984. This time, her childhood friend Kathryn Sullivan made history by becoming the first American woman to walk in space.

Sally Ride has shared her exciting experiences and knowledge in books for kids, including *To Space and Back* in 1986 (written with Susan Okie) and *Voyager: An Adventure to the Edge of the Solar System* in 1992 (with Tam O'Shaughnessy).

LEARN MORE! READ THESE ARTICLES...
ASTRONAUTS • MOON • SPACECRAFT

DID YOU KNOW?

Other "female firsts" in space include Valentina Tereshkova of Russia (formerly the Soviet Union), the very first woman in space (1963), and Mae Jemison, the first African American woman astronaut, aboard the space shuttle *Endeavor* (1992).

SEARCH LIGHT

True or false? Sally Ride is famous for being the first woman in space.

Before Sally Ride became the first American woman in space, she was part of the team on the ground, communicating with the astronauts in space. It must have been exciting to experience both sides of those calls.

© Bettmann/Corbis

Answer: FALSE. She is famous for being the first *American* woman in space.

Exploring the New Frontier

Once the Moon was the only important thing in **orbit** around planet Earth. Today many objects circling the Earth have been launched into space by human beings. All these orbiters, including the Moon, are called "**satellites**." Those launched by people are called "**artificial** satellites."

Communications satellites send telephone, television, and other electronic signals to and from places on Earth. Weather satellites take pictures of the clouds and wind systems. Various scientific satellites gather information about outer space. There are even "spy" satellites to take pictures for the military. And there are space stations.

In the late 20th century the United States, Russia, the European Space Agency, Japan, and Canada joined forces to build the International Space Station (the ISS). It is meant to have people on it all the time. In 1998 the first two ISS **modules** were launched and joined together in space. In November 2000 the first three-person crew, an American and two Russians, occupied the still-growing station.

Large space stations are planned for the future. These will have many people working in them all the time. They may be like airports are today, where a person changes planes to go to a specific destination. But from a spaceport people would change spacecraft to travel to the Moon, another planet, or another space station.

LEARN MORE! READ THESE ARTICLES...
ASTRONAUTS • MOON • PLANETS

DID YOU KNOW?

In order to leave the Earth's gravity and visit a space station, you must travel at a speed of 7 miles per second.

SEARCH LIGHT

Why is a space station called a satellite?

In November 2000 the first three-person crew, an American and two Russians, occupied the still-growing International Space Station.
© NASA

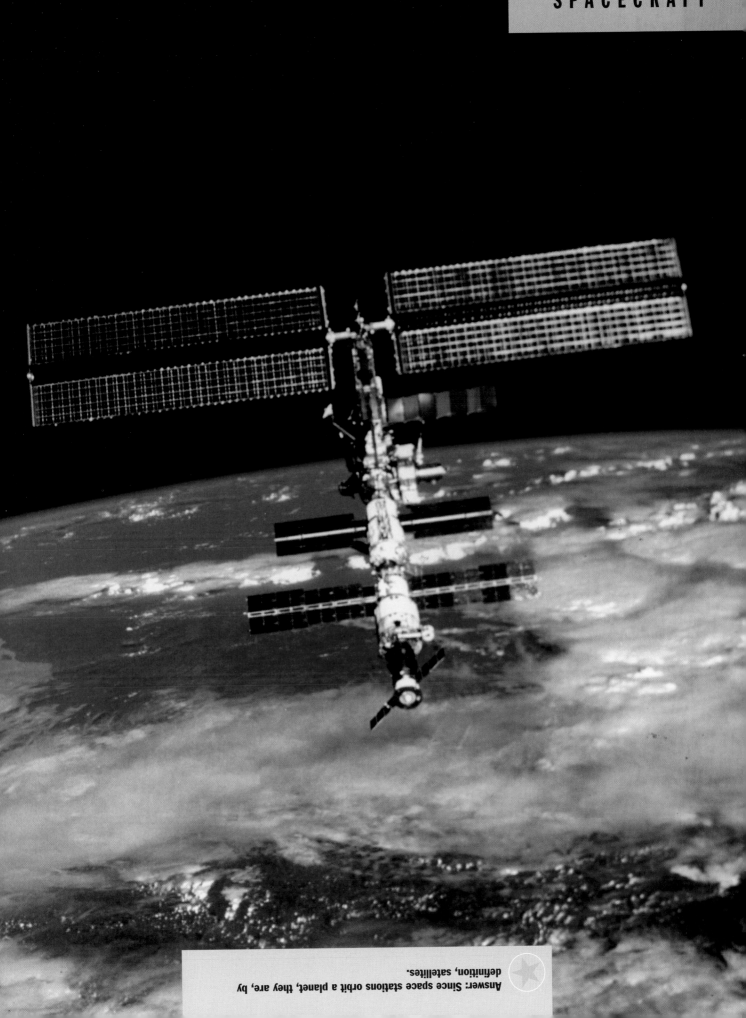

Going Up in Space

Space is what we call the area that's 100 miles or more above Earth's surface. Below that boundary is Earth's **atmosphere**—the layer of gases including the air we breathe. In space there is no air to breathe. And it is very, very cold.

Russia and the United States were the first countries to send people into space. Russia's space travelers are called "cosmonauts," which means "space sailors." Those from the United States are called "astronauts," meaning "star sailors."

In 1961 cosmonaut Yuri Gagarin became the first man to travel into space. In 1969 U.S. astronaut Neil Armstrong became the first man to walk on the Moon. Sally Ride, in 1983, was the first American woman astronaut.

Today people travel into space inside **space shuttles** that ride piggyback on a rocket into space. After blastoff, the Earth outside the shuttle moves farther and farther away until it looks like a big blue-and-white sea outside the astronauts' window.

In space anything not tied down will float—including the astronauts themselves! Earth's gravity has become too weak to hold things down. In fact, it's hard to tell what "down" means in space.

The shuttle's many special machines help astronauts exist in space. The main computer helps fly and control conditions within the shuttle. A long metal arm lets the astronauts handle things outside their ship. And many other machines are carried along for experiments.

Today most space shuttle trips are to space stations, where astronauts and cosmonauts can live while they work in space.

LEARN MORE! READ THESE ARTICLES...
GRAVITY • SALLY RIDE • SPACECRAFT

DID YOU KNOW?
Because different planets have different gravities, an astronaut's weight would change from planet to planet. For example, an astronaut weighing 165 pounds on Earth would weigh only 62 pounds on Mars but 390 pounds on Jupiter.

SEARCH LIGHT

Space is the area
a) more than 100 miles out from Earth.
b) more than 10 miles out from Earth.
c) more than 1,000 miles out from Earth.

Imagine you are lying on your back inside a space shuttle. Two long rockets will help your heavy spaceship get off the ground. With five seconds to go, the fuel in your spaceship starts burning. "Five...four...three...two...one."
NASA

Answer: a) more than 100 miles out from Earth.

Life Beyond the Earth

Could there be life elsewhere in the universe? There are some people who think that it's possible. They have given the idea a name, extraterrestrial life. "Extra" means "beyond" and "terrestrial" means "of the Earth," so altogether the name means "life beyond the Earth."

Most scientists believe that for another planet to have life on it, it must have an **atmosphere** (air), light, heat, and water like the Earth does.

We get our light and heat from the Sun. The universe is filled with millions of stars like our Sun. Scientists are trying to find out if these stars have planets, maybe Earth-like planets. If there is such a planet, then it could have life on it.

It's not easy to find extraterrestrial life. The universe is an immense place to search. Some scientists believe that if there is intelligent life elsewhere, it may send radio signals to us. So far, the only signals that scientists have found are the natural ones that come from stars and planets themselves.

SEARCH LIGHT

In addition to an atmosphere, which three things are needed for life?
a) water, heat, and air
b) dirt, heat, and light
c) water, heat, and light

Whether it is possible or not, the idea of beings on other planets has excited people for years. Some believe that aliens from other worlds have even visited Earth. They call these aliens "extraterrestrials," or "ETs." Some even claim to have seen ETs and their spaceships, which are called "unidentified flying objects," or simply "UFOs."

What do you think, are there creatures living on other planets? And how do you think they would live?

LEARN MORE! READ THESE ARTICLES…
ASTRONAUTS • SPACECRAFT • UNIVERSE

Answer: c) water, heat, and light

G L O S S A R Y

agriculture farming

artificial made by human beings rather than occurring in nature

atmosphere the envelope of gases that surrounds a planet

axis imaginary pole going through the center of the Earth or other heavenly body

chemical one of the combined substances making up living and nonliving things

comet chunk of frozen space debris that has a shiny tail and orbits the Sun

crater bowl-shaped dent in a surface

cratered marked with bowl-shaped dents

data factual information or details

debris trash or fragments

diameter the length of a straight line through the center of an object

eclipse darkening of the Sun, Moon, or other heavenly body by the shadow of another heavenly body

element in science, one of the simplest substances that make up all matter

expanse large area

graduate school higher-level university program available to students who have completed the basic study program

gravity force that attracts objects to each other and keeps planets circling the Sun

imperial having to do with an emperor or empire

investigate look into or study

laboratory place where science tests and experiments are done

massive heavy or large

meteorite a mass of material from space that reaches the Earth's surface

module independent unit made to be part of a larger structure

molecules the smallest possible pieces of a particular substance

monitor watch carefully and keep track of

orbit (verb) travel around an object; (noun) an object's path around another object

particle tiny bit

phenomenon (plural phenomena) event or happening

photoelectric effect electrical effect produced when light strikes a metal surface

prism a piece of many-sided clear crystal

rotate spin or turn

rotation spinning or turning

satellite natural or man-made object that circles another object, usually a planet

space shuttle rocket-launched airplane-like vehicle that transports people to and from space

sphere ball or globe

supernova the explosion of a very large star during which it may become a billion times brighter than the Sun

Portland Community College